"Just as I thought — not as far advanced as ourselves..."

The hole that got away.

The follow through...

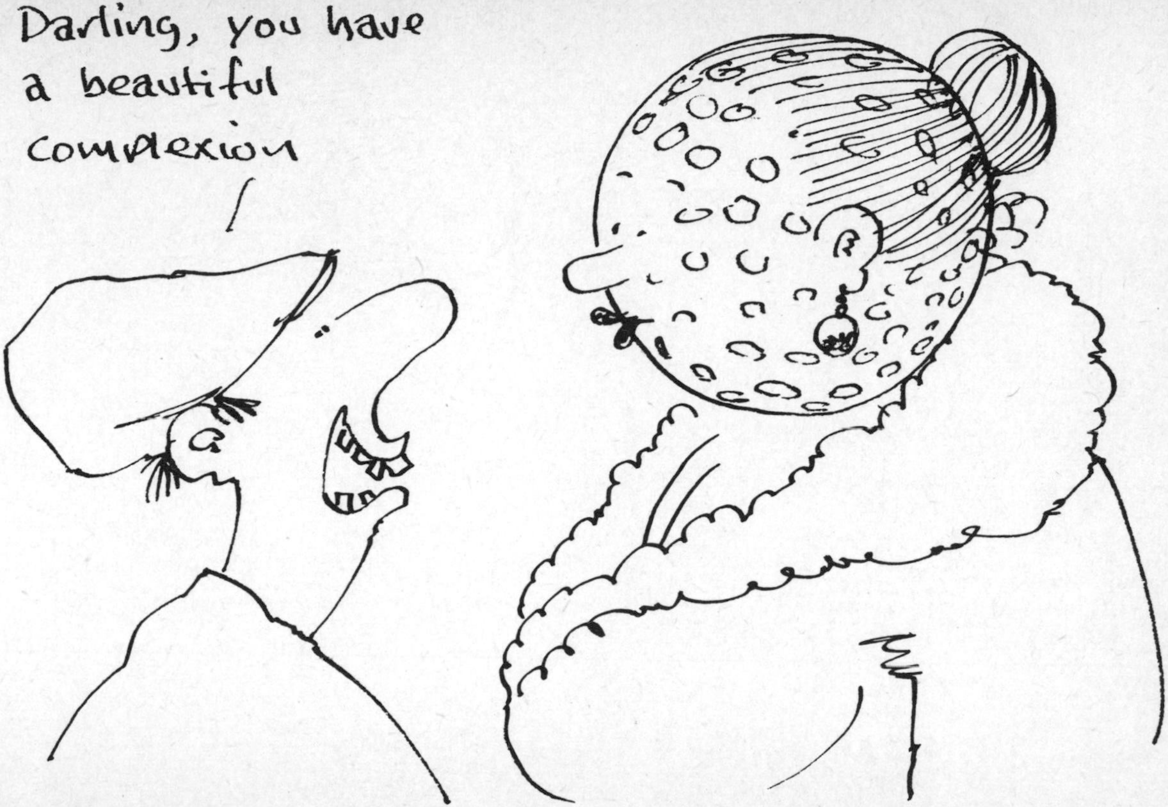
Darling, you have a beautiful complexion

"Oh, and I'll need some clubs —
those nice blue & gold ones will match my outfit."

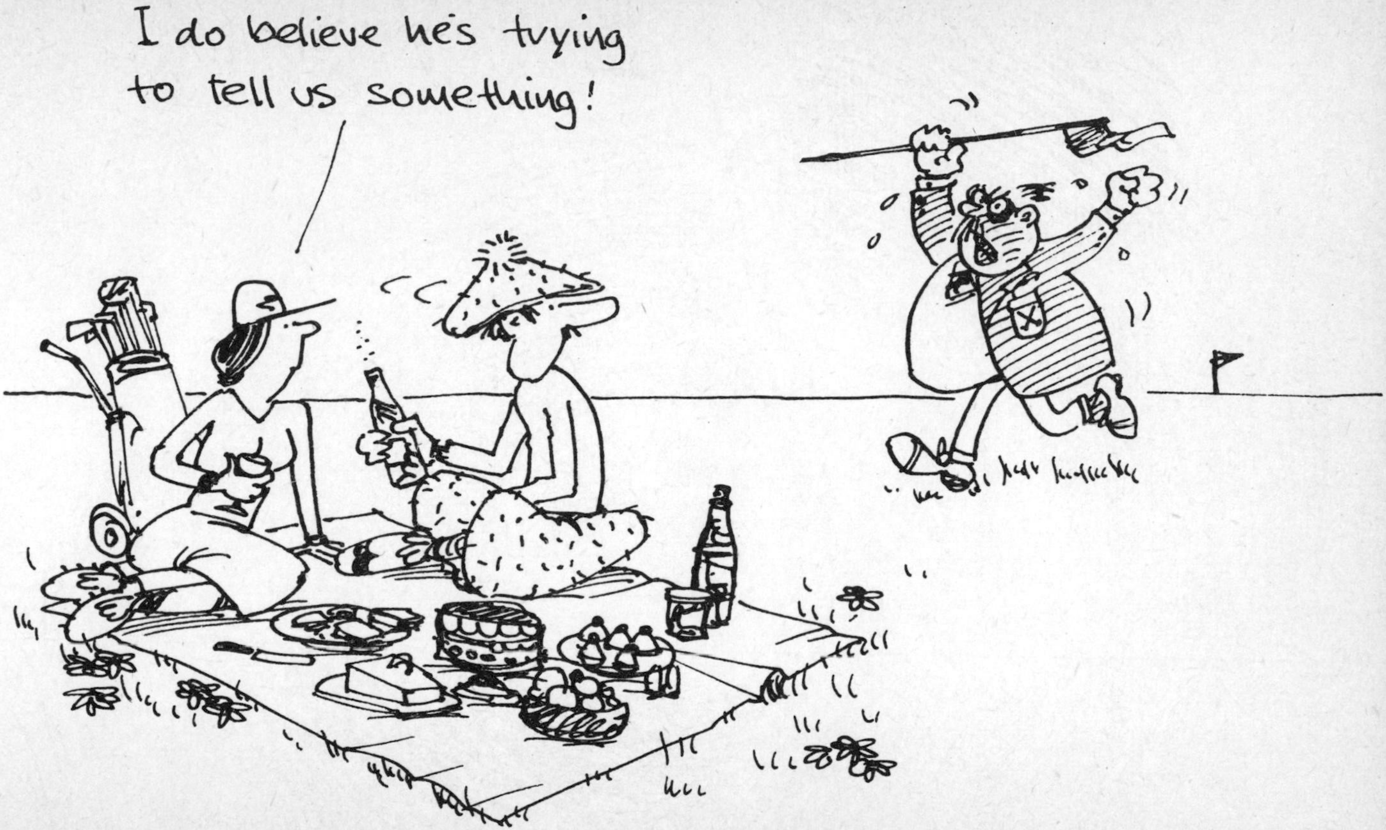
I do believe he's trying to tell us something!

Ah! you've found my ball!

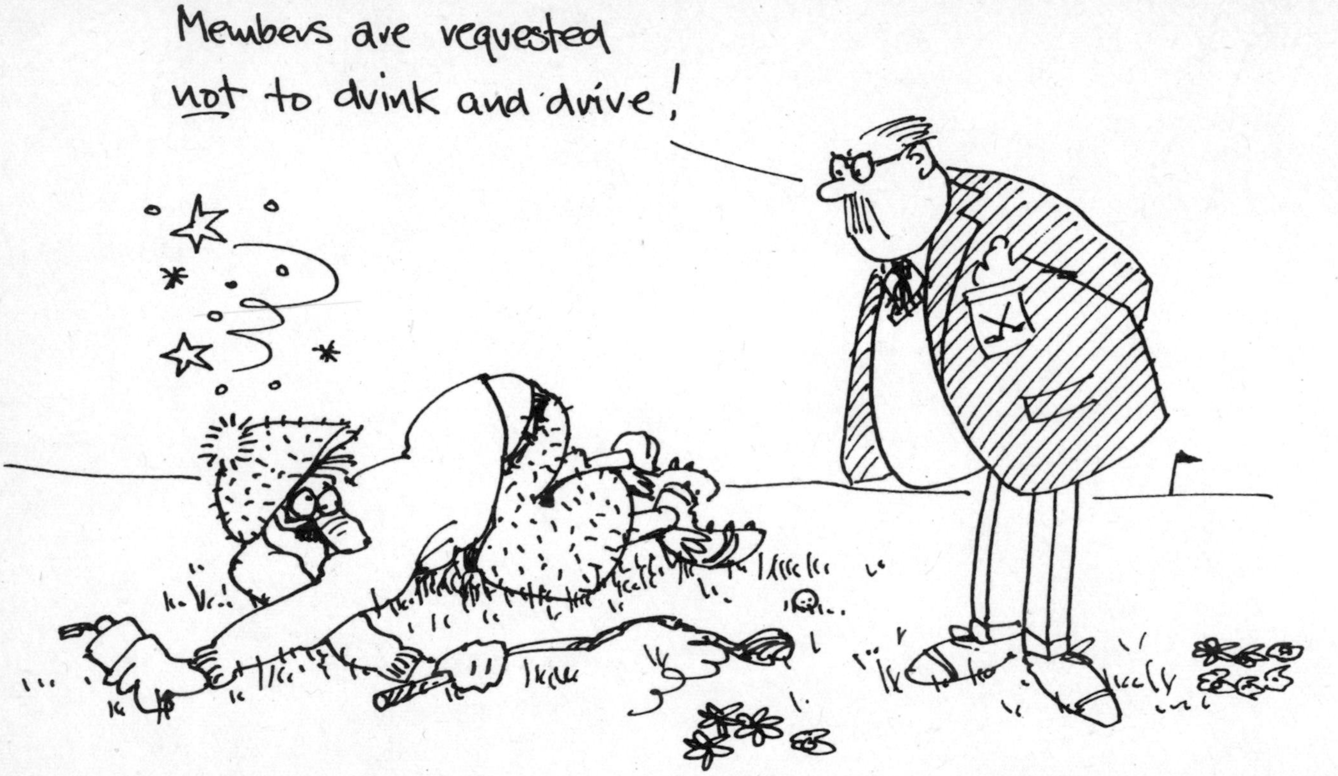
Members are requested not to drink and drive!

Remember to replace pin at all times when leaving the green.

Bunker Shot.

I got them cheap off Ronnie Corbett.

Dealing with a Water Hazard.

"I'm damned sure you forfeit a stroke for this!"

How to deal with the Golf Club Bore.

My God — Another U.F.O. Now do you believe me!

Out of bounds...

... in the
rough...

The .38 Iron.

I always dress to suit the game I expect from my opponent!

A wee saving on Caddie fees...

A distraction to a lady's game ...

... the problem solved!

Improving your game.

"Look at those silly sods - fishing in this weather!"

... be considerate to others ...

You there— have you seen
a golf ball land near here?

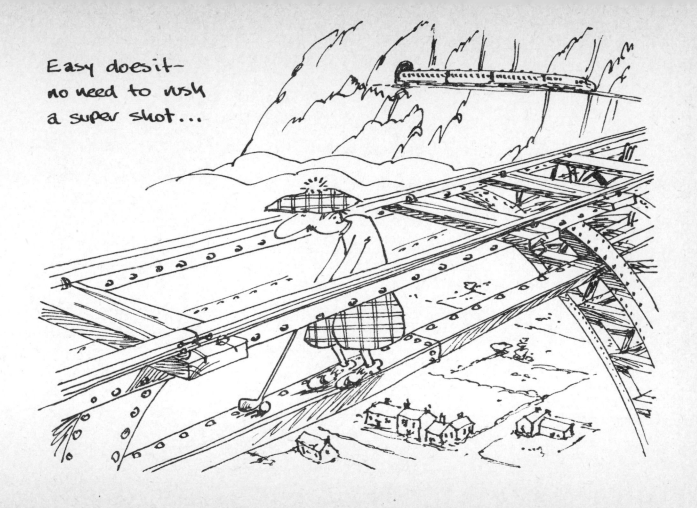

Divine Intervention...